Nourish

A Beginner's Guide to a Plant-Based Lifestyle

By: Janae Horton

Youtube: Young Boodhas   Instagram: @jae_organics   Facebook: Live inc.

This publication contains the opinions and ideas of its author. It is intended to provide helpful and informative material on the subject addressed in the publication. It is sold with the understanding that the author is not engaged in relaying medical, health-care, or any other kind of professional services in the book. The reader should consult his or her own competent medical, health-care, or other professional before adopting any of the suggestions in this book or drawing references from it.

The author specifically disclaims all responsibility for any liability, loss, or risk, personal or otherwise, which is incurred as a direct or indirect consequence of the use and application of any of the content of this book.

Live Inc.
Interested in booking Janae Horton for an event? Visit live4ever.org/contact for more information.

Copyright (C) 2018 by Janae Horton
All rights reserved, including the right to reproduce this book or portions thereof in any form whatsoever.

Photography done by RH ImageNation.
For more information regarding photography, contact RH ImageNation at ray@rhimagenation.com

Manufactured in the United States of America

Acknowledgments

I would like to express my deepest gratitude to everyone who supported me in the creation of this book. Thank you to my parents, for loving me and creating the space that has allowed me to follow my dreams. Thank you, RH Image Nation, for producing all of the beautiful images in this book. Finally, thank you, dear reader, for purchasing this book. I pray that you have a long, healthy, heart-filling, meaningful, and prosperous life.

Table of Contents

Introduction..7

Nutrition Education

American Health Statistics..9
Benefits of a Plant-Based Diet..10
How to Nourish Yourself 11

Cooking Tips

Meal-Plan...15
Different Types of Salt 17
Different Types of Cooking Oils...18
How to Cook Dried Foods..19

Smoothies

Cream Shake...23
Caribbean Sunshine..24
Sweet Sunrise Juice..25
Tropical Green..26
Daterade..27

Salads

Harvest Salad..30
Curry Salad...32
Southwest Salad 34
Cabbage Salad..36
Berry Salad...37

Soups

Southwest Black Bean Soup...40
Lentil Soup..43
Spicy Vegan Chili...44
Veggie Zoodle soup..47
Vegetable Plate...48

Healthy Alternatives

Quinoa Fruit Bowl..53
Breakfast Skillet..54
Jamaican Porridge..56
Stuffed Peppers..57
Guacamole...58
Plantain Fries...60
Chili Lime Snow Peas..63
Garlic & Thyme Mashed Potatoes.......................................64
Balsamic & Garlic Spinach..65
Black Bean Dip..66
Roasted Vegetables...67
Sweet Plantains...68
Sautéed Kale...69

Sweet Treats

Berry Nice Cream..72
Sweet Rolls..75
Date Snickers..76
Coco Dates..77

Indulge

Apple & Date Oatmeal...80
Veggie Toast..83
Veggie Sub..84
Veggie Quesadilla..87
Bella Burger...88
Panang Curry Vegetables..90
Caribbean Asian Fusion Stir-Fry..91

Additional Resources

GMO Information..96
Do Your Own Research..97
Citations...98

Introduction

Welcome to the world of *Live*

In these pages, I share recipes, cooking tips, and detailed scientific breakdowns of the major nutrients that your body needs. If you're interested in learning more about a plant-based lifestyle, you'll also find information about a number of helpful resources. When I was in college, I didn't expect to transition to a mainly plant-based diet—honestly, it just kind of happened.

I started off like most college students: young, hopeful, and unsure of my future path. After bouncing around a few different majors, I finally settled on nutrition science, and just like that, I was hooked! Before the switch, eating was something I never put much thought into; it was basically a mindless habit. After I became a nutrition science major, my perspective about the foods I ate completely changed. My eyes had been opened, and the world of food suddenly looked so different to me. I realized that the foods we eat directly affects our health, and I began to see food as medicine.

This sparked an interest to do more research outside of the classroom. I learned so much as I pored over the latest peer-reviewed research and ultimately discovered a mantra: "if you want to sustain life, you must eat life". This notion led me down the rabbit hole of plant-based nutrition, and now, I'm all in! Of course, my personal commitment to a mainly plant-based lifestyle doesn't mean the same is true for you. You are the expert of your own life, and therefore know what works best for you. Although a strictly plant-based diet may not seem appealing, you can receive a lot of benefits by simply incorporating more plant-based meals into your life.

I hope you'll learn from this book, explore beyond it, and embrace the delicious plant-based foods to improve your body, your mind, and the way you LIVE!

Love,

Janae Horton

Nutrition Education

We cannot achieve optimal health or get perfect beach-ready bodies without understanding how our bodies function. In order to succeed on our healthy journey we must understand where we are collectively, as a people, in terms of health; why plant-based meals are a healthier option; and what nutrients our bodies need to thrive. In this section, I will touch on all of these aspects, providing you with the tools you need to understand the mechanics of your own body.

American Health Statistics

Assessing Americans' Health

According to a 2015 US Centers for Disease Control and Prevention (CDC) study, the leading cause of death in the United States is heart disease. Heart disease can be attributed to our dietary habits and other lifestyle factors like smoking, drinking, and stress. In 2014, more than two out of every three adults were considered to be either overweight or obese,[1] and today, more than a third (>36.5 percent) of the US population is considered obese.[2] Consequently, obesity is a risk factor for chronic diseases, like diabetes, heart disease, stroke, and some types of cancer. What does this boil down to? In short, a significant percentage of Americans are ending their lives prematurely and suffering from various chronic diseases due to their dietary choices. If you are interested in learning more about the causes and consequences of obesity, check out the page on this topic on the CDC's website, www.cdc.gov/obesity. This amazing resource will help you and your loved ones remain informed about the dangers of obesity.

What are We Eating?

Now that we know the number-one cause of death in the US is related to diet, and that more than a third of the population is obese, an obvious question arises: How did this happen? What are we eating, or not eating, that is causing this diet-related epidemic?

According to a study done by the US Department of Agriculture (USDA), most Americans are not following the recommendations put forth in its publication, Dietary Guidelines for Americans 2015–2020, Eighth Edition.[3] On average, most Americans consume too many processed grains and foods that are high in fat and too few fruits and vegetables. Another component to consider is sugar. The average American unknowingly consumes about 19.5 teaspoons of sugar each day; compare that to the American Heart Association's recommended guideline, a maximum of 6 tsp/day for women and 9 tsp/day for men. These dietary habits conspire to play a key role in the explosion of overweight and obesity among Americans, and countless untimely deaths attributed to diet-related diseases.

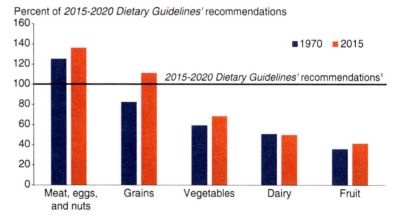

Estimated average U.S. consumption compared to recommendations, 1970 and 2015

[1]Based on a 2,000-calorie-per-day diet.
Loss-adjusted food availability data are proxies for consumption. Rice availability data were discontinued and thus are not included in the grains group.
Source: USDA, Economic Research Service, Loss-Adjusted Food Availability Data and 2015-2020 Dietary Guidelines.

Benefits of a Plant-Based Diet

"Eating more fruits and vegetables adds nutrients to diets, reduces the risk for heart disease, stroke, and some cancers, and helps manage body weight when consumed in place of more energy-dense foods."

- Center For Disease Control and Prevention [4]

As young children, we are taught to eat our fruits and vegetables. We all know this to be true, but most Americans have chosen to ignore this advice. Now, as awareness of the prevalent health problems arise, it's time to make a shift towards eating more of them.

A collection of compelling evidence exists that proves increased consumption of fruits and vegetables can lower the risk of chronic diseases, such as heart disease and stroke. The Harvard University School of Public Health conducted the largest and longest study on this topic to date; the study included almost 110,000 men and women whose health dietary habits were followed for 14 years.[5] The researchers found a correlation between increased consumption of fruits and vegetables and decreased risk of cardiovascular disease among study participants. Therefore, it's reasonable to assume that if we all increased our consumption of fruits and vegetables, fewer of us would become overweight and suffer from diet-related diseases. Many studies have also shown that a plant-based diet can improve digestion, sleep, vitality, physical and mental health, blood sugar levels, cholesterol levels, emotional states, and increase energy levels.[6]

In 2013, the informative article "Nutritional Update for Physicians: Plant-Based Diets" was published in the peer-reviewed official journal of Kaiser Permanente.[7] The following are three important quotes from the article that I would like you to keep in mind throughout your health and wellness journey.

1. " Healthy eating may be best achieved with a plant-based diet, which we define as a regimen that encourages whole, plant-based foods and discourages meats, dairy products, and eggs as well as refined and processed foods."
2. " Too often, physicians ignore the potential benefits of good nutrition and quickly prescribe medications instead of giving patients a chance to correct their disease through healthy eating and active living."
3. "Physicians should consider recommending a plant-based diet to all their patients, especially those with high blood pressure, diabetes, cardiovascular disease, or obesity."

How to Nourish Yourself on a Plant-Based Diet

In order to achieve the best results possible from a plant-based diet, you must have a clear understanding of what nutrients your body needs, as well as the food, herb, or seasoning sources you can get them from. The nutrients your body requires to function properly can be broken down into two categories: macronutrients and micronutrients.

Macronutrients

Macronutrients are specific nutrients that must be consumed from dietary sources in large quantities to provide the body with energy for growth and maintenance. The energy that our body requires is measured in calories. Most of our calories should come from macronutrients, which are broken down into three categories: carbohydrates, fats, and proteins.

Carbohydrates. For some reason, many people hate carbohydrates. A common misconception dictates that carbs are the cause of weight gain, and many believe that high-carb diets are unhealthy. I'm here to tell you that this belief is not true. In reality, carbohydrates are the most important macronutrient available and should make up about 45-65% of our diet. This nutrient is vital because it is needed to fuel the body and brain.

Therefore, those who go on a low-carb diet to lose weight may experience symptoms of fatigue or headaches, because they are depriving their body and brain of its primary source of energy. Each gram of carbohydrates provides the body with 4 calories of energy.

The huge misunderstanding regarding carbs is centered around the difference between simple and complex carbohydrates. Most people consume too many simple carbohydrates, such as sugar and refined grains, and this overconsumption contributes to weight gain and high blood sugar levels. These carbohydrates have been broken down into their simplest form, and as such, they have been stripped of most, and sometimes all, of their vital nutrients. Consequently, these foods will provide you with calories to sustain your hunger while causing a blood sugar imbalance inside your bloodstream.

Complex carbohydrates, on the other hand, are not processed; therefore, they remain in their complete form, retain their nutrients, and take a longer time to be broken down by the body. Because complex carbs require more time to be broken down, they do not cause a substantial spike in blood sugar levels. Healthy sources of complex carbohydrates include fresh fruits and vegetables; whole grains, such as quinoa, spelt flour, teff flour, wild rice, barley, kamut flour, etc., nuts. and seeds.

11

Fat. Food-based fats are the components of foods that do not dissolve in water. The fats in foods are broken down into a few categories: oils, fats, and related compounds, such as cholesterol. Fats are typically solid at room temperature, while oils are liquid. All fats and oils are concentrated sources of energy and provide the body with 9 calories per gram.

Although fat is the densest macronutrient, you should not fear it. Fats should make up about 20 to 35 percent of your daily diet. They play a vital role in many important bodily functions, including cholesterol and sex hormone synthesis, the construction of cells (as components of cell membranes), transport of fat-soluble vitamins, and production of essential fatty acids, which are required for growth and good health.

Essential fatty acids found in fat include the omega-6 and omega-3 fatty acids. Ironically, many Americans suffer from heart disease due to the overconsumption of omega-6 fatty acids, which are known as "bad fats" and can contribute to the clogging of arteries and inflammation in the body. These fats are mainly found in animal-based foods, such as meat, dairy, eggs, etc. Healthy omega-3 fatty acids are found in fish and other plant-based sources, such as nuts (walnuts); seeds (Chia, flax, hemp); avocados; nut oils; dark green leafy vegetables (Brussels sprouts); and vegetable oils (algal, Perilla).

Protein. Protein is another category of macronutrients, and its coverage in the media is extremely misleading. Stories often encourage high-protein diets for weight loss and muscle building. There is some truth to this claim, but not as much as you might think. It is true that the body needs protein to build and maintain tissue (i.e., muscles, red blood cells, and so on), and it is also true that the body can use protein as an energy source. However, protein is not our body's preferred source of energy. Similar to carbohydrates, protein provides the body with 4 calories per gram. Although this is the same amount of energy (aka calories), protein takes a longer time to be converted into energy and produces a different end-product. This is why proteins should only make up about 10 to 35 percent of your diet.

In addition, high-protein diets often become high-fat diets, because most people assume that animal-based foods are the best sources of protein. This misconception can lead to the overconsumption of foods like chicken, fish, and eggs. Like red meat, these foods are high in fat and can increase your risk of developing chronic disease. The best sources of protein are plant based, because they're low in fat and loaded with vital nutrients. Healthy plant-based sources of protein include quinoa, beans, lentils, legumes, chia seeds, and hemp seeds.

Micronutrients

Micronutrients are also vital to good health, but they are required in smaller quantities. Micronutrients can be broken into two main categories: vitamins and minerals. These nutrients are so important, and luckily most of them are easily consumed daily in the foods that we already eat. Therefore, I have compiled a small list of vitamins and minerals that people who follow a strict plant-based diet typically do not get enough of. I have also provided you with some information regarding why these nutrients are so important and where you can get them from.

Vitamin B-12. Required for proper red blood cell formation, neurological function, and DNA synthesis, vitamin B-12 is typically found in animal-based foods, including meat, fish, poultry, dairy, and eggs. It is generally not present in most plant foods except two forms of edible algae: dried green and purple seaweed (nori). Fortified cereals are another readily available source of vitamin B-12. The most reliable source for those following a strictly vegan diet, however, is a dietary supplement. Simply follow the instructions on the package and you will ensure that your body has enough of this important vitamin.

Vitamin D. An important vitamin for bone, digestive, and overall metabolic health, vitamin D is best obtained via sunlight. 15 minutes of natural sunlight each day will provide your body with a lot of natural benefits. It is a fat-soluble vitamin, so to receive the most benefits, you need to ensure that you are consuming a good amount of healthy fats along with daily exposure to natural sunlight. Although natural sunlight is the best source of vitamin D, a daily dietary supplement is also a good alternative.

Iron. This mineral helps red blood cells transport oxygen and nutrients to all of the cells in the body. Unfortunately, iron deficiency is the most common nutrient deficiency in North America. The best plant-based sources of iron includes lentils, lima beans, quinoa, fortified cereals, oatmeal, pumpkin seeds, squash, pistachios, sunflower seeds, tomato sauce, swiss chard, collard greens, and prune juice.

Calcium. Many people believe that you must consume dairy in order to get enough dietary calcium, but that's purely a myth. Calcium is a mineral found in soil, so it's absorbed by the roots of plants; animals get enough calcium by consuming these calcium-rich plants, and so can we. Calcium is extremely important for bone health, so make sure you get enough of it in your diet. Certain greens are very rich in calcium, but all whole plants contain some calcium. Excellent plant-based sources of calcium include Chinese mustard greens, bok choy, kale, white beans, collard greens, navy beans, mustard spinach, and Chinese cabbage. If you are still concerned about consuming enough calcium then you should consider a dietary supplement.

Phosphorus. This nutrient is extremely important for proper cell function, maintenance of strong bones and teeth, regulation of calcium, and production of adenosine triphosphate (ATP). Some scientific research suggests that phosphorus is more easily absorbed when consumed in meat products, and that you only absorb half of the phosphorus contained in plant foods. As such, it's important to either consume a daily dietary supplement of this mineral or incorporate a large amount of phosphorus-rich foods into your diet. These foods include pumpkin seeds, Brazil nuts, adzuki beans, yellow beans, white beans, chickpeas, black turtle beans, pinto beans, and kidney beans.

Zinc. It's is not found in large amounts in plant-based foods, but according to research, vegetarians and omnivores alike have similar levels of this mineral. The best plant-based sources of zinc are garbanzo beans, pinto beans, kidney beans, lentils, almonds, walnuts, pistachios, pecans, peanuts, sunflower seeds, peas, oatmeal, and chia seeds.

Cooking Tips

This section offers a guide to help you lose weight as well as cooking tips that allow you to choose the best types of ingredients that work for you! In addition, you will learn how to cook dried ingredients that are soft and infused with delicious flavor!

Weight-loss Meal Plan

Our lives are so busy and hectic that we often don't realize the weight that we gain over time until its too late. Boom! We are 10-30 pounds heavier, we know it, everybody else knows it, and we are stuck wondering what to do. We often times become so desperate to get fast results that we will try unhealthy fad diets, weight-loss supplements, temporarily join a gym, or just say "forget it" and give up. Trying to make a lifestyle change alone, without the proper education and social support can be very difficult and discouraging.

Thankfully this guide will make your journey to weight-loss so much easier. The three-sisters weight-loss guide that I have developed is guaranteed to give you fast and lasting results. While completing this guide you will enjoy a smoothie for breakfast, salad for lunch, and soup for dinner. The recipes that I have developed are healthy, tasty, and will help you lose weight fast! This system works because all of the recipes are low in processed and refined grains, preservatives, sugar, and fat, which we have now learned, have more than twice as many calories as carbs and proteins. These foods are not included in the plan because they promote weight gain and inflammation in the body. Therefore, by following this guide, you will fill your body with good carbohydrates it needs for fuel, protein to repair and build muscles, healthy fats to keep your hormones in balance, and vital vitamins and minerals to keep you well nourished and energized. This guide is not about depriving your body or taste buds, it is all about nourishing every cell in your body with delicious plant-based foods. In order to get the best results from this plan, please follow all of the guidelines listed below. If you are interested in additional support, contact me to learn more about health coaching and how I can help you stick to your goals!

Weight-loss Guidelines

1. Drink 16 oz. of water prior to drinking your smoothie.
2. Drink at least 1/2 your bodyweight in oz. of distilled water every single day. For example, if you weigh 140 lbs., you need to drink 70 oz. of water. This is the minimum amount of water that you need to properly flush your body of excess toxins and keep your cells hydrated so they can perform optimally. You can consume room temperature water, ice water, boiled water with lemon or lime, or fruit infused water. DO NOT add sweeteners or packets to your water.
3. Drink a smoothie for breakfast every morning. If you become tired of drinking smoothies, refer to the healthy alternatives section for other breakfast options.
4. Eat a salad for lunch. You can either meal prep and eat the recipes in this book, or you can buy a salad at a restaurant or grocery store. Make sure that the salad is 100% vegan (including the dressing). If you're tired of eating salads, refer to the healthy alternatives section for plant-based sides that you can mix and match to create a delicious and healthy meal.
5. Eat a soup for dinner. Similar to the salad, you can use the recipes in this book or buy a soup. Again, just make sure that the soup is 100% vegan. You can also refer to the healthy alternatives section for sides to mix and match to create a healthy dinner.
6. If you get hungry in between your meals, either consume water, eat 1-2 pieces of fresh fruit, or eat a handful of nuts.
7. You can have 1 cheat meal/dessert each week. Choose this treat from either the sweet treat or indulge section of this cookbook.
8. Perform a breathwork exercise each day for 2-10 minutes. Inhale allowing the belly to fully release, exhale pulling the belly button to the back of your spine. Doing this each day will increase the amount of oxygen in your body promoting an alkaline state and burning stubborn fat in the body. Stop performing the exercise if you begin to feel dizzy or light headed.
9. Do some form of moderate exercise for 30 minutes 3+ times each week.
10. Get at least 6-8 hours of sleep each night.
11. If interested, meditate daily and choose one of the following mantras to state each day. This will help you get your mind right!

Mantras and Meditation

Stating a mantra everyday as well as mindful meditation helps us re-wire our brain. If this is something that interests you, choose a mantra below to state daily. If none of these mantras inspire you, feel free to create your own! When meditating, simply find a quite location, close your eyes, and focus on the feeling of air entering and leaving your mouth or nostrils. If your mind begins to wander, bring your awareness back to the breath. This mindfulness exercise will help you regain control of your brain and allow you to consistently focus on the goals that you have created for yourself. Meditate for 5-30 minutes each day.

I eat to nourish my cells.

My health is improving and so is my life.

Healing is happening in my body and mind.

I aim for progress not perfection. 90% fuel, 10% fun.

Everything I eat and drink heals me and nourishes me.

Trusting and loving my body is becoming easier and easier.

Letting go of the past is good for me. It is safe for me to let go.

I can do this. I am doing this. Healing is happening right now.

I can heal my body. I am healing my body. My body is healing.

I am guided by my intuition. I know what to eat and how to live my life.

I love myself and my life. I naturally connect with other like-minded and positive people.

I can feel that everything is beginning to change. I am feeling healthy, focused, and determined.

I love the process of improving my health. I am feeling healthier and stronger with each day that passes.

A treat does not have to be something that I eat. I love rewarding my self by (insert options). Examples: going to the spa, getting my nails done, going to the movies, etc.

Different Types of Salt

Salt is one of the most common seasonings that we use. We use it so often that we take it for granted and only use it to add flavor to our food. Certain types of salts have more uses than just adding flavor to foods, some salts are rich in important minerals that our body needs to function. In this book I do not specify the type of salt to use, I simply state salt. I leave that choice up to the discretion of each individual reader. Below I have given you some information about some of the most commonly used salts so you can make the best choice for you and your family.

Table Salt
Table salt, the most commonly consumed salt, is highly refined, with most of the trace minerals removed in the process. It is also treated with a caking agent to keep it from clumping. I used this salt for many years, but now that I know about its impurities and lack of nutrients, I no longer keep it in my kitchen.

Kosher Salt
Kosher salt is less refined than table salt. It's flakes are much coarser, so a little can go a long way.

Sea Salt
Sea salt, which is harvested from evaporated sea water, is usually unrefined and is therefore much coarser than table salt and kosher salt. Since it is unrefined, it contains many vital minerals, including zinc, potassium, and iron. These minerals enhance the flavor of the salt, making it much more complex and robust than both table and kosher salt.

Himalayan Pink Salt
This salt is my favorite! Pink Himalayan salt, considered to be the purest form of salt in the world, and it is harvested from the Khewra Salt Mine in the Himalayan mountains of Pakistan. It contains up to 84 natural minerals and elements that are also found in the human body, and its rich mineral content gives it an even bolder flavor than sea salt.

Different Types of Oils

There are so many different oils to choose from! I've learned a lot about them, and below, I recommend the oils I believe are best used raw and those I cook with. Of course, ultimately, you will make your own decisions. Additionally, when preparing these recipes, try to use the least amount of oil possible. This is necessary because oil is simply liquid fat, so cutting out excess oil will also cut out some excess calories. You'll notice in the recipes that I sometimes substitute water for oil when cooking, as I find it to be a healthier option when sautéing vegetables. With that being said, use oil sparingly, and incorporate healthier plant-based oils into your life!

Oils to Use Raw

I like to use coconut and olive oil in its raw form. When these oils are heated excessively, they undergo a chemical reaction that converts them from a good fat to bad fat—with the potential to raise your cholesterol and blood pressure levels. Since this is the case, I like to use these oils to make salad dressing or raw treats.

Oils for Cooking

Grapeseed, avocado, hemp seed, and sesame oils are my favorites for cooking; they are more stable and are not subject to the same chemical reactions as the oils listed above. Grapeseed oil is my go-to option because it's relatively flavorless, compared to the other options.

Best Ways to Cook Dried Foods

Barley & Quinoa

When cooking quinoa or barley you should generally follow a 3:1 ratio. This means that for every cup of grains you should use 3 cups of water.

Steps

1. In a bowl, cover the grains with water and set aside to soak for 1 to 2 hours prior to cooking.
2. Drain the grains. In a large pot with a lid over medium-high heat, bring the cooking water to a boil.
3. While waiting for the water to reach a boil, line the inside of the pot's corresponding lid with aluminum foil.
4. Once the water has reached a boil, add the drained grains to the pot.
5. Stir the mixture for about 30 seconds and then reduce the heat to low. Cover and simmer for about 12 to 15 minutes.
6. Remove the lid and check the texture of the grains. If they are thoroughly cooked, remove from the heat and serve. If all of the water has evaporated and the grains are still hard, add a small amount of water to the pot, cover, and cook for another 3 to 5 minutes.
7. Repeat, checking the grains periodically until they are cooked to the desired texture. Remove from the heat and serve.

Beans, Legumes, & Lentils

Add 2 to 3 whole cloves of garlic and a chopped onion to the pot to infuse your beans or lentils with flavor.

Steps

1. Soak the beans or lentils for several hours. Overnight is best, but if you don't have much time, soak them for at least 2 to 3 hours.
2. Drain the beans or lentils. Place them in a large pot with a lid. Completely cover the beans or lentils with water and place the pot over high heat.
3. Watch the pot carefully. Once the water reaches a boil, reduce the heat to medium-low, cover, and simmer for 15 to 20 minutes.
4. Periodically check the texture of the beans by tasting them. Once they have reached the desired texture, remove from the heat and serve.

Smoothies

Start your day off right with these nutrient rich and delicious smoothies. These high-carb drinks are easy to take on the go and will satisfy your body with enough energy to fuel you through your busy mornings!

Cream Shake..23
Caribbean Sunshine..24
Sweet Sunrise Juice...25
Tropical Green...26
Daterade...27

Cream Shake

Serves 1

So sweet, so creamy, and so satisfying! This smoothie is so decadent and simple, it's honestly one of my favorites. Not only is it a great source of iron, fiber, healthy fat, vitamin D, vitamin E, and magnesium; but it tastes soooooo good! This recipe is a crowd pleaser, share it with family and friends!

Ingredients
10 dates
3/4 cup almond milk
1/4 cup rolled oats

Directions
1. Remove the seeds from all of the dates.

2. Add all of the ingredients into a blender and blend until evenly combined.

3. Serve and enjoy!

4. For added flavor, garnish your smoothie with cinnamon and granola.

Tips

Love Overnight Oats? Refrigerate this drink overnight to get the same thick and creamy texture.

Need Fresh Almond Milk?
1. Soak 1 cup of almonds in filtered water for 24 hours.

2. Add 1 cup of almonds, 3 cups of water, 1 tsp vanilla extract, and 2 dates into a blender.

3. Blend the mixture until all of the ingredients are evenly combined.

4. Strain the ingredients through a cheesecloth.

5. Store the almond milk in the refrigerator for later use.

Caribbean Sunshine

Serves 1

This sweet and spicy smoothie will make your skin glow! It's high in vitamin C and other nutrients with anti-inflammatory properties that help increase skin regeneration and soothe inflammation. Create your own little paradise at home and glow from the inside out!

Ingredients
1 cup frozen mango
1 cup coconut water
1/4 cup frozen pineapple
1-inch ginger
1 tsp chia seeds

Directions
1. Remove the skin from the ginger.

2. Toss all of the ingredients into the blender and blend on the highest setting until evenly combined.

3. Serve and enjoy!

Tips

Love a good smoothie bowl? Add this smoothie to a small bowl and garnish it with your choice of toppings! My favorites are fresh fruit, dried fruit, coconut shreds, sliced almonds, and granola.

Sweet Sunrise

Serves 1

Got Manganese? This delicious smoothie is full of it! This nutrient is often forgotten, but is super important! It plays a major role in bone health, the production of collagen in the skin, regulates blood sugar, and protects the body against free radical damage. Enjoy this smoothie knowing that you are protecting your body and slowing the aging process.

Ingredients
3 dates
1 cup frozen mango
1 cup fresh strawberries
1 cup fresh raspberries
3/4 cup filtered water
1/2 cup unsweetened cranberry juice
1 tsp chia seeds

Directions
1. Remove the pit from dates.

2. Toss all of the ingredients into a blender.

3. Blend the ingredients on the highest setting until the juice is smooth and evenly combined.

4. Serve and enjoy!

Tropical Green

Serves 1

The classic green smoothie! This smoothie has gained a lot of fame over the years for being nutrient rich and surprisingly delicious. This recipe has a twist that will help your body absorb even more nutrients, thanks to our little friend the avocado. Avocados are a healthy source of fat and helps your body absorb the fat-soluble vitamins in your food. So enjoy this smoothie knowing that you're absorbing as much vitamin K and A as possible!

Ingredients
2 handfuls spinach
1/2 avocado
1 cup filtered water or coconut water
2 dates
1 cup frozen mango
1 cup dole frozen mixed fruit

Directions
1. Add the spinach, avocado, and water into the blender. Blend on the highest setting until it is evenly combined.

2. Remove the pit from the dates.

3. Add the dates, mango, and mixed fruit to the blender and blend again on the highest setting until the smoothie is evenly combined. Serve and enjoy!

Daterade

Serves 1

Sweetened with natural sugars, this drink is light, smooth, and loaded with iron. Drink this in the morning or prior to a workout for a boost of energy.

Ingredients
10 medjool dates
1 apple
2 cups water
2 **pinches** cinnamon
1/4 inch ginger

Directions
1. Remove the seed from all of the dates, the core from the apple, and skin from the ginger.

2. Toss all of the ingredients into the blender and blend on the highest setting until evenly combined.

3. Serve and enjoy!

Tips

Need something more filling? Mix in 1/4 cup of dried oats, and allow it to sit in the fridge overnight. This will create delicious overnight oats.

Need more protein? Mix in 1/4 cup of chia seeds, and allow it to sit in the fridge overnight. This will create sweet chia pudding.

Salads

Lunch time is usually the busiest time of the day; so eating something healthy can sometimes be tricky. These recipes keep that in mind—they're easy to meal prep and take with you on the go. Enjoy these delicious green, and mostly raw recipes at work, school, or in the comfort of your own home.

Harvest Salad	30
Curry Salad	32
Southwest Salad	34
Cabbage Salad	36
Berry Salad	37

Harvest Salad

Serves 4

This savory roasted butternut squash salad is the eptiome of Autumn. This hearty and fiber-rich salad will leave you full and satisfied.

Ingredients

4 cups butternut squash, diced
2 tbsp grapeseed oil
1/2 tsp pink himalayan salt
1/2 tsp roasted garlic and herb seasoning
2/3 cup barley, dried
1 cup kale
1 cup lettuce
1/4 cup red onions
1/8 cup nuts of choice

1/8 cup dried cranberries

Directions

1. Pre-heat oven to 425 degrees Fahrenheit.

2. Add diced butternut squash to a large mixing bowl. Add in oil, salt, pepper, and roasted garlic and herb seasoning.

3. Toss the mixture around until the squash is evenly coated in oil and seasonings.

4. Spread the squash onto a baking sheet lined with parchment paper or aluminum foil. Allow it to cook in the oven for 15 minutes on each side

5. Prepare the dried barley. Follow the instructions on package or the directions on page 19 of this book.

6. Chop the kale, lettuce, and red onion to desired size. Add these ingredients, nuts, and dried cranberries to a large bowl.

7. Once the barley and squash are prepared, remove them from the heat and allow them to cool.

8. Add 1/4 cup of squash and 1/8 cup of barley to your salad. Store the rest of the cooked ingredients for later use.

9. Serve your salad and enjoy with your choice of salad dressing.

Tips

Need a good salad dressing? Use the recipe for the balsamic vinaigrette on page 37. It pairs well with this salad

Curry Salad

Serves 4

This salad is inspired by the classic Jamaican combination of curry, plantains, and cabbage. These ingredients are so good that I had to combine them all into one bowl.

Ingredients
1 **clove** of garlic
1/2 onion
1/2 tomato
1/2 bell pepper
grapeseed oil, as needed
3/4 cups cooked garbanzo beans
3 tbsp curry powder
1/2 tsp turmeric
1/2 tsp cumin
1/2 tsp jamaican jerk rub
1 dash coriander
1 dash allspice
1/2 cup coconut milk
1/2 cup water
1/2 tsp pink himalayan salt
1/2 tsp black pepper
1 dash cayenne pepper

Toppings
2 plantain
2 avocado
2 tomato
1 head of green cabbage

Directions

1. Slice the garlic, onion, green pepper, and tomato to desired size.

2. Pour enough cooking oil into a medium-sized pan to thinly coat its bottom, place over medium/high heat.

3. Add garlic, onion, and tomato to the pan. Cook for about 3-4 minutes or until fragrant.

4. Add cooked garbanzo beans, green peppers, curry powder, turmeric, cumin, jamaican jerk rub, coriander, and allspice to the pan. Turn the stove down to medium/low heat. Continue to stir the mixture and cook for about 2-3 minutes.

5. Stir in coconut milk, water, cayenne pepper, black pepper, and pink salt. Cover the mixture with a lid and let it simmer for about 20 minutes over medium/low heat. Continue to stir the mixture periodically to prevent the ingredients from sticking to the pan.

6. Pour enough oil to thinly coat the bottom of a separate small pan. Place the pan over medium/high heat and allow the oil to warm.

7. Slice plantains into thick strips (about ¼ inches thick). Add them into the pan and cook each side for about 3-4 minutes or until each side has reached a golden brown color. Once the plantains are cooked, remove them from the heat and allow them to drain onto a plate lined with paper towel.

8. Slice avocado, raw cabbage, and tomato. Add the desired amount to a medium-sized salad bowl and store the rest for later.

9. Once the chickpeas have finished cooking, remove them from the heat and add about 3-4 tablespoon to your salad. Also add in the desired amount of sliced plantain and enjoy!

Tips

Love this combination but tired of eating salads? Wrap all of these ingredients in a collard green leaf or tortilla shell and enjoy a delicious curry burrito.

Southwest Salad

Serves 1

This plant-based spin on the infamous taco salad is loaded with enough ingredients and flavors to satisfy both your stomach and your taste buds.

Ingredients
grapeseed oil, as needed
3 cloves garlic
1/2 onion
1 tbsp jerk seasoning
1/2 tsp black pepper
1/2 tsp pink Himalayan salt
1/2 cup cooked black beans
1 handful cherry tomatoes
1/4 cucumber
1 handful lettuce
1 handful kale
2 tbsp guacamole
salsa, as needed
cilantro lime dressing
(or dressing of choice), as needed

Directions
1. Pour enough cooking oil into a small pan to thinly coat its bottom, place it over medium heat. Chop the garlic and onions and add them into the pan. Cook until the onions become translucent.

2. Add jerk seasoning, black pepper, and pink Himalayan salt. Stir and cook the ingredients for about 1-2 minutes or until fragrant.

3. Add the cooked black beans to the pan, and continue to stir the ingredients around until the beans are warm and evenly coated.

4. Remove the black beans from the pan and allow them to cool.

5. Slice the tomatoes, cucumber, lettuce, and kale to the desired size. Combine all of these ingredients and black beans into a large bowl.

6. Top your salad with guacamole, salsa, and your choice of salad dressing.

7. Serve and enjoy!

Tips

Need a fresh guac recipe? Check out page 58.

Cabbage Salad
Serves 1

This delicious salad is full of important micronutrients including Vitamin K, Vitamin C, and Vitamin B12.

Ingredients
2 cups green cabbage
1 cup red cabbage
1 green onion
1/2 tomato
1/4 avocado
1/4 cucumber
1/8 cup carrot
ginger dressing, as desired

Directions
1. Chop all of the ingredients to the desired size. Dice the green onion and only use the green leafy section for your salad.

2. Add all of the chopped ingredients into a large salad bowl and enjoy with your choice of dressing.

Berry Salad

Serves 1-2

This crisp, light, and refreshing salad offers the perfect blend of sweet and savory flavors.

Ingredients
1/2 cup olive oil
1/3 cup balsamic vinegar
1 clove garlic
1 tbsp agave syrup
1/2 tsp pink himalayan salt
1/2 tsp black pepper
1 dash dijon mustard
1 handful kale
1 handful arugula
1 handful tomatoes
1 handful blackberries
1 handful dates
1 handful strawberries
2 tbsp sliced almonds

Directions
1. Prepare the salad dressing by adding the olive oil, balsamic vinegar, dijon mustard, garlic, pink salt, agave syrup, and black pepper into a blender. Blend all of the ingredients until the dressing is evenly mixed.

2. Prepare the salad by chopping all of the produce to the desired size and placing them in a large plate or bowl. Top the salad with your homemade dressing, sliced almonds, and garnish with your choice of dried fruit.

Soup

Everyone loves to commune over a great-tasting meal. Share these delicious soup recipes with the ones you love. After all, nothing says "I love you" more than a healthy and delicious meal cooked with love.

Southwest Black Bean Soup...................40
Lentil Soup..43
Spicy Vegan Chili....................................44
Veggie Zoodle soup................................47
Vegetable Plate.......................................48

Southwest Black Bean Soup — Serves 4

I promise you that this soup tastes way better than it looks! Serve it with a slice of avocado toast and enjoy the beautiful blend of flavors!

Ingredients
1/2 tsp coriander
2 tsp pink himalayan salt
1 tsp black pepper
1 tsp fresh cilantro
1/2 tsp Mrs. Dash's garlic and herb seasoning
2 pinch cumin
1 pinch paprika
1 pinch cayenne pepper
3 cups vegetable broth
1 cup water
1 tomato
1 onion
4 cups cooked black beans
3/4 cup salsa
1 slice Ezekiel bread, toasted
avocado, as needed

Directions
1. Blend all of the seasonings together in a food processor. (including coriander, salt, black pepper, cumin, garlic and herb seasoning, paprika, cayenne pepper, cilantro).

2. Add the vegetable broth and water into a large pot over medium-low heat.

3. Slice tomato and onion to preferred size. Add the blended seasonings, tomato, and onion to the pot and allow the mixture to reach a light boil.

4. Add the salsa and cooked beans to the soup. Taste the soup and add additional seasonings to taste. Cover the soup with a lid and allow it to simmer for 10-15 minutes.

5. Remove the soup from the heat and allow it to cool.

6. Pour the soup into a blender and blend it on the lowest setting for about 30-45 seconds.

7. Serve the soup with a slice of avocado toast topped with pink Himalayan salt, black pepper, and cayenne pepper for those who want an extra kick.

Tips

Love toppings? Garnish your soup with fresh avocado slices, red onions, and cilantro.

Lentil Soup

Serves 5

Don't settle for a bland lentil soup. Make it right and you will have everyone begging for more! Enjoy this warm and savory soup with the ones you love.

Ingredients
1 onion
1-2 cloves garlic
1/2 tsp coriander
1 tsp black pepper
1 tsp pink himalyan salt
1/2 tsp rotisserie chicken rub
2 pinch cumin
3 cups vegetable broth
4 cups cooked lentils

Directions
1. Slice the onion and garlic to desired size.

2. Blend the coriander, black pepper, salt, rotisserie chicken rub, and cumin in a food processor.

3. Pour vegetable broth into a large pot and place it over medium/high heat. Add the seasonings, onion, and garlic to the pot. Allow the broth reach a light boil.

4. Add in the cooked lentils. Turn the stove down to low heat and allow it to simmer for about 10-15 minutes.

5. Serve the soup in your favorite bowl and enjoy!

Tips

For a smoother texture, blend the soup on the lowest setting for about 30-45 seconds.

Spicy Vegan Chili

Serves 5

This is going to be the best vegan chili you've ever made! It is hearty, spicy, and jam-packed with flavor!

Ingredients
- **2** yellow onions
- **4 cloves** garlic
- **1 large** green pepper
- **1 large** red pepper
- **1** jalapeño
- **4 tbsp** grapeseed oil
- **2 tbsp** chili powder
- **1 tbsp + 1 tsp** cumin
- **1 tsp** dried oregano
- **1 tsp** smoked paprika
- **1 tsp** garlic and herb seasoning
- **1 tsp** pink himalayan salt, plus extra to taste
- **1 tsp** Blue Mountain Jamaican Spicy Curry
- **1/2 tsp** allspice
- **1/2 tsp** Chipotle Roasted Garlic seasoning
- **1 cup** corn, fresh or frozen
- **1 can** spicy chili beans
- **1 cup** black beans, cooked or canned
- **1 cup** lentils, dried
- **2.5 cups** veggie broth
- **2 cups** crushed tomatoes, fresh or canned

Directions
1. Dice the yellow onions, garlic, green pepper, red pepper, and jalapeño.

2. Add cooking oil to a large pot over medium-high heat. Allow the oil to heat up.

3. Add onions to the pot and cook for 3-5 minutes. Stir periodically.

4. Add garlic, green pepper, and red pepper to the pot and cook down for an additional 2-3 minutes.

5. Add all of the seasonings to the pot and continue to stir the vegetables for another 2-3 minutes allowing them to soak up the herbs and spices.

6. Add jalapeños, corn, chili beans, black beans, and lentils to the pot. Stir the mixture around for a minute.

7. Add veggie broth and crushed tomatoes to the pot. Stir the mixture periodically and allow it to reach a light boil.

8. Once the mixture has reached a boil, turn down the stove to the lowest setting, place a lid on the pot, and allow it to simmer for 30-35 minutes or until the beans have reached the desired texture.

9. Remove the chili from the heat and allow it to cool.

10. Serve with your choice of toppings and enjoy!

Tips

Too spicy? Ditch the jalapeños and replace the spicy chili beans with mild chili beans. Also you can garnish your soup with avocado slices or mix in some of your favorite plant-based milk.

Veggie Zoodle Soup

Serves 3-4

This asian inspired zoodle soup is so savory and comforting! Enjoy the blend of bold flavors any day of the week!

Ingredients

3 zucchini
2 carrot
2.5 bell peppers
2 onions
1 red potato
1/2 large sweet potato
1 cup snap beans
1 cup mushrooms
4 cloves garlic, minced
1/2 inch ginger, minced
6 cups of vegetable broth
1 cup coconut milk
3 tbsp red thai curry paste
1 tbsp jamaican curry powder
1 tsp pink himalayan salt

Directions

1. Slice the bell peppers, onions, red potato, sweet potato, snap beans, and mushrooms to the desired size. Use a spiralizer to spiralize the carrot and zucchini.

2. Mince the garlic and ginger. Place a large pot over medium-high heat.

3. Add enough vegetable broth to lightly cover the bottom of the pot. Add the garlic, ginger, and onions to the pot. Cook until the onions become translucent.

4. Add potatoes, sweet potatoes, curry paste, curry powder, salt, coconut milk, and the rest of the vegetable broth to the pot. Stir the pot and allow the potatoes to cook for 10-12 minutes.

5. Add the bell peppers, snap beans, and mushrooms to the pot, and allow the soup to cook for an additional 6-8 minutes.

6. Add the zucchini and carrots to the pot and allow the soup to cook for an additional 2-3 minutes.

7. Remove the pot from the heat, and serve the soup in a small bowl. Enjoy!

Veggie Plate

Serves 3

This plate of veggies is quick and easy to make. Devour this beautiful blend of flavors and nutrients.

Ingredients

2 peeled sweet potatoes
2 red skin potatoes
1 yellow onion
1 red pepper
grapeseed oil, as needed
Mrs. Dash Garlic and Herb seasoning, as needed
black pepper, as needed
pink himalayan salt, as needed
4 tbsp agave syrup
1 tsp cinnamon
1 dash nutmeg
1 cup spinach

Directions

1. Pre-heat oven to 400 degrees Fahrenheit

2. Slice sweet potatoes, red skin potatoes, red pepper, and onion to desired size.

3. Place red skin potatoes in a small bowl. Add 1 tablespoon of olive oil, 1 teaspoon of garlic and herb seasoning, 1 teaspoon black pepper, 1/2 teaspoon pink salt. Toss the potatoes around in the bowl until the potatoes are evenly coated in oil and seasonings.

4. Remove the potatoes from the bowl and spread them onto a baking sheet lined with parchment paper. Place the potatoes into the oven.

5. Mix agave syrup, cinnamon, nutmeg, and 2 teaspoons olive oil in a small mixing bowl. Use a basting brush to brush the mixture onto all sides of each sweet potato. Place the sweet potatoes onto a baking sheet lined with parchment paper.

6. Put the sweet potatoes into the oven. Periodically brush the sweet potatoes with the sweet sauce every 10 minutes. Allow the potatoes to cook for about 25-35 minutes or until they have reached the desired texture

7. Pour enough water into a medium-sized pan to barely cover its bottom and place it over medium-high. Add 1 teaspoon pink salt, 1 teaspoon black pepper, and sliced onions into the pan. Cook until the onion becomes translucent.

8. Add the peppers to the pan and cook for about 4-5 minutes or until they become tender.

9. Add spinach and cook until the spinach has wilted. Remove the vegetables from the heat.

10. Remove the potatoes from the oven and serve all of these delectably seasoned vegetables together on one plate.

Healthy Alternatives

Tired of eating the same foods? Learn the secret to making amazing and healthy plant-based meals. Create one of these appetizing breakfast options or mix and match your favorite side dishes to make delicious a rewarding lunch/dinner.

Breakfast Options
Quinoa Fruit Bowl...53
Breakfast Skillet...54
Jamaican Porridge...56

Mix & Match Lunch/Dinner Options
Stuffed Peppers..57
Guacamole..58
Plantain Fries...60
Chili Lime Snow Peas..63
Herb Mashed Potatoes..64
Balsamic & Garlic Spinach................................65
Black Bean Dip..66
Roasted Vegetables...67
Sweet Plantains...68
Sautéed Kale..69

Quinoa Fruit Bowl

Serves 4-5

A tangy twist on the traditional fruit salad. Enjoy this high carb, high protein meal for several mornings in a row

Ingredients
1 cup water
¼ cup quinoa
1 cup strawberries
1 cup blueberries
1 cup blackberries
1 cup mango
¼ cup agave syrup
2 tbsp lime juice

Directions

1. Pour the water into a large pot over high heat. Allow the water to reach a boil.

2. Add the quinoa to the water, stir briefly, for about 30 seconds. Turn the stove down to low heat and place a lid on the pot allowing the quinoa to simmer. Cook the quinoa for about 20-30 minutes, or until it has reached its desired texture.

3. Once the quinoa is cooked, drain it and allow it to cool.

4. Slice all of the fruit to desired size, and place them in a large bowl.

5. Mix the agave syrup and lime juice together in a small bowl.

6. Combine the cooked quinoa, chopped fruit, and sauce together in a large bowl.

7. Serve the desired amount in a small bowl and eat up!

Breakfast Skillet

Serves 3

This is my favorite breakfast recipe! It has a delectable blend of flavors. If you love savory, sweet, or anything citrus, this is the perfect meal for you!

Ingredients
grapeseed oil, as needed
1 plantain
water, as needed
1/2 tsp pink himalayan salt
1/2 tsp black pepper
1/2 tsp jerk seasoning
1/2 yellow onion
1/2 green pepper
1/2 red pepper
1 cup spinach
1 tbsp guacamole

Directions
1. Pour enough oil into a large pan to thinly coat its bottom and place over medium-high heat. Place the plantain slices into the oil and cook each side for about 3-4 minutes or until the plantain turns a dark brown color. Once the plantains are cooked, remove them from the pan and place on to a paper-towel lined plate to drain and cool.

2. Slice the peppers, onions, and mushrooms to the desired size.

3. Pour enough water into a medium-sized pan to lightly cover the bottom. Add the seasonings to the water and allow the water to reach a light boil. Place the vegetables into the pan and allow them to cook until the onions are translucent. Add the spinach into the pan and cook until the spinach has wilted.

4. Serve this tasty dish by placing the cooked veggies on a plate and topping them with your cooked plantains and pre-made guacamole

Tips

Need Fresh Guac? Turn to page 58 to find a fresh guacamole recipe.

Leftover veggies? Add the veggies to your favorite soup recipe and save the plantain for the curry salad on page 33.

Jamaican Porridge

Serves 2

This recipe is inspired by my loving grandma. She made it for my cousins and I all the time when we were growing up. If you love oatmeal, this smooth and creamy spin-off is calling your name!

Ingredients

2 cups water
1 cup oatmeal
1/4 tsp pink himalayan salt
1/2 cup coconut milk
1 tsp vanilla
1/2 tsp cinnamon
1 dash of nutmeg
4 tbsp agave syrup
3 dates
1 banana
Toppings of choice: fruit, nuts, coconut shavings, etc.

Directions

1. Pour the oatmeal, water, and salt into a medium-sized pot over medium/high heat. Allow the mixture to reach a boil. Stir periodically to create an even mixture.

2. Once the mixture has reached a boil, reduce the heat and let it simmer for about 5 minutes. Continue to stir constantly.

3. Stir in coconut milk, vanilla, cinnamon, and nutmeg. Cook for about 1 more minute.

4. Finally, stir in the agave syrup.

5. Remove the porridge from the heat, and allow it to cool for 2-3 minutes.

6. Add the oatmeal, 3 pitted dates, and 1 banana to a blender.

7. Blend the mixture until it reaches a smooth and creamy texture.

8. Pour the porridge into a bowl and garnish with your choice of fresh fruit, sliced nuts, or coconut shavings.

Stuffed Peppers

Serves 2

This crisp and crunchy taco will trick your taste buds into thinking you're actually eating meat. Try it out for yourself!

Ingredients

2 small cloves garlic
1/2 cup walnuts
1/8 cup tamari sauce
1/8 cup olive oil
1 tsp cumin
1 tsp onion powder
1/2 tsp black pepper
1/2 tsp pink himalayan salt
1/2 tsp coriander
2 dash cayenne pepper
1 dash paprika
2 large sweet peppers
Guacamole, as needed
Salsa, as needed

Directions

1. Add all of the seasonings and walnuts into a food processor and pulse for 1-2 minutes or until the walnut meat has reached its desired texture.

2. Slice the peppers in half and remove the stem.

3. Fill the peppers with the desired amount of walnut meat, guacamole, and salsa.

Guacamole

Serves 3

This classic snack is great and so easy to make. Serve this delicious dip with fresh veggies, plantain chips, or anything else that your heart desires.

Ingredients
- **1-2 cloves** garlic
- **1/2** tomatoes
- **1/4** red onion
- **1/8** cup fresh cilantro
- **2** avocados
- **1/2** lime
- **1/2** tsp pink himalayan salt
- **1/2** tsp black pepper

Directions
1. Slice tomatoes, red onion, cilantro and garlic cloves to desired size.

2. Slice the avocados in half and remove the seed and peel. Add the avocado into a medium-sized mixing bowl.

3. Use a fork to mash the avocado to desired texture.

4. Add chopped vegetables and seasonings into the bowl.

5. Stir the guacamole until evenly mixed.

6. Serve this delicious dip with your choice of ingredients or incorporate it with another dish.

Tips

Want an extra kick? Spice up your guacamole by adding a dash of ground cayenne pepper or half of a jalapeño pepper

Got Guac? Add it to one of the following meals:
Southwest Salad..........................34
Breakfast Skillet..........................54
Stuffed Peppers..........................57
Vegan Quesadilla.......................87

Plantain Fries

Serves 1

Unripe plantains are a great substitute for potatoes. Enjoy this delicious, oil free, and guilt-free French fry recipe.

Ingredients
1 unripe yellow plantain
1/2 tsp pink himalayan salt
1/2 tsp pepper
condiment of choice

Directions
1. Preheat oven to 400 degrees Fahrenheit.

2. Cut the ends off of the plantain.

3. Slice the plantain in half, and slice each piece down the middle. Do not remove the skin from the slices.

4. Continue to cut the plantains into strips keeping the skin in tact.

5. Line a baking sheet with aluminum foal or parchment paper.

6. Place each slice of plantain onto the sheet with the skin down on the tray to prevent the plantains from sticking.

7. Sprinkle salt and pepper onto the plantain strips.

8. Bake for 15-20 minutes.

9. Remove the plantains from the heat, remove the skin, and allow them to cool.

10. Serve with your choice of condiment!

Chili Lime Snow Peas
Serves 1

This is for everyone that loves a little spice. Remix your life with this blend of spicy and citrusy flavors.

Ingredients
water, as needed
1-2 cloves of garlic
1 tsp pink himalayan salt
1 tsp of crushed red peppers
1/2 tsp black pepper
1 handful snow peas
1/2 lime

Directions
1. Pour enough water into a small-sized pan to lightly cover its bottom. Turn the stove on medium-high heat and allow the water to reach a light boil.

2. Finely mince the garlic as small as you can possibly get it.

3. Add garlic and seasonings to the water. Allow it to simmer for less than a minute.

4. Add snap beans to the pan and stir frequently. Cook the snow peas for about 3-4 minutes or until the peas have reached the desired texture

5. Remove the snow peas from the pan and allow them to cool.

6. Squeeze lime juice over the snow peas prior to serving.

Herb Mashed Potatoes

Serves 3

These creamy garlic and thyme mashed potatoes are fluffier than ever and will not go to waste. The serving size for this side is 2 tablespoons/day so please don't overdo it! Enjoy this dish with 2 non-starch sides.

Ingredients
2 red-skin potatoes
water, as needed
4 sprigs fresh thyme
2 cloves garlic
1 tbsp vegan butter
1/8 cup vegetable broth
1 tsp pink himalayan salt
1/2 tsp pepper
1/2 tsp garlic powder
1/2 tsp onion powder

Directions
1. Add the potatoes to a medium-sized pot filled with water, and place the pot over medium-high heat. Use enough water to completely cover the potatoes.

2. Allow the potatoes to reach a boil. Continue to cook the potatoes for an additional 20-25 minutes.

3. Remove the potatoes from the pot and allow them to cool.

4. Dice 2 cloves of garlic and strip the leaves from the sprigs of thyme.

5. Add the vegetable broth, vegan butter, garlic, thyme, salt, pepper, garlic powder, and onion powder into a medium-sized pot. Place it over medium-low heat.

6. Add the cooked potatoes to the pot, and use a potato masher or fork to mash the potatoes to the desired texture.

7. Add the mixture to a food processor or blender to get a smoother/creamier texture.

8. Remove the mashed potatoes from the food processor, serve and enjoy!

Black Bean Dip

Serves 2

This warm and hearty dip is great to snack on alone or with others. Enjoy this delicious dip with plantains chips or side of choice.

Ingredients
1 cup cooked black beans
1 tsp coriander
1 tsp cumin
1 tsp pink himalayan salt
1/2 tsp black pepper

Directions
1 Pour cooked black beans into a large mixing bowl.

2. Mash the black beans with a fork or use a food processor.

3. Add seasonings to the mashed beans and mix the dip until even combined.

4. Serve and enjoy!

Tips

Too dry? If the dip is too dry when blending, add in a little bit of vegetable broth or your favorite plant-based milk.

Blend the dip in a blender or food processor for a smoother texture.

Protein rich spread? Spread this dip onto a sandwich or slice of toast!

Balsamic Garlic Spinach

Serves 2-3

These flavorful greens are tender and delicious. This recipe has a high concentration of chlorophyll which helps to cleanse the blood. Savor your meal while nourishing your body

Ingredients
2 cloves of garlic
1/2 tomato
1/4 red onion
grapeseed oil, as needed
1/8 cup balsamic vinegar
1/2 tsp pink himalayan salt
1 tsp garlic and herb seasoning
2 cups spinach

Directions
1. Dice garlic, tomato, and red onion.

2. Add enough cooking oil to lightly cover the bottom of a medium-sized plan. Place the pan over medium-high heat.

3. Add the garlic, tomato, and red onion to the pan. Cook for 3-4 minutes.

4. Add the balsamic vinegar, salt, and garlic and herb seasoning to the pan. Stir to create an even mixture.

5. Add the spinach to the pan, and cook until the spinach has wilted.

6. Remove the spinach from the heat. Serve and Enjoy!

Roasted Vegetables

Serves 2

These warm, savory, and tender vegetables are delicious. Consume a variety of veggies with this quick and simple recipe

Ingredients
1 bell peppers
1 delicata squash
1 yellow onion
1 zucchini
1 tbsp grapeseed oil
1 1/2 tsp roasted garlic seasoning
1 tsp minced garlic
1/2 tsp black pepper
1/2 tsp zatar seasoning
1 dash pink himalayan salt

Directions

1. Pre-heat the oven to 400 degrees Fahrenheit.

2. Slice the vegetables to desired size and add them to a medium-sized bowl.

3. Add cooking oil, roasted garlic, minced garlic, black pepper, and zatar to the bowl.

4. Toss the veggies around until they are all evenly coated with oil and seasoning.

5. Line a baking pan with aluminum foil or parchment paper.

6. Add the vegetables to the pan, spreading them out as evenly as possible.

7. Bake 20-25 minutes or until it has reached desired texture. Periodically use a spatula to move the veggies around while they are cooking.

8. Remove the veggies from the oven. Sprinkle a dash of salt across the veggies and serve!

Sweet Plantain

Serves 2

Baked sweet plantains are a household favorite. These plantains are extremely healthy and compliment any savory dish.

Ingredients
1 yellow plantain
1/8 cup grapeseed oil
1 tsp coconut sugar
1/2 tsp cinnamon
1 dash nutmeg
1 dash pink himalayan salt

Directions

1. Pre-heat the oven to 350 degrees Fahrenheit.

2. Cut the ends off of the plantain.

3. Remove the skin, and slice the plantains at an angle into thick sections.

4. Add the slice plantains, cooking oil, and seasonings into a large mixing bowl.

5. Stir or toss the ingredients until the plantains are evenly coated with oil and seasonings.

6. Line a baking pan with parchment paper or aluminum foil. Spread the plantains onto the pan making sure not to crowd the plantains.

7. Bake for 7 minutes on each side.

8. Remove the plantains from the heat, allow them to cool, and enjoy!

Sautéed Kale

Serves 2

This side dish is nutrient rich and flavorful. Enjoy this savory and oil-free dish with any side of your choice!

Ingredients
2 cups kale
2 cloves garlic
1/4 yellow onion
1 tsp smoked paprika
1 tsp roasted garlic and herb seasoning
1/2 tsp pink himalayan salt
1 dash black pepper
1/8 cup water

Directions
1. Dice the cloves of garlic and yellow onion.

2. Add the water to a medium-size pan over medium heat.

3. Add the garlic and onions to the pan. Cook until the onions become translucent.

4. Add the seasonings and chopped kale to the pan.

5. Cook the kale until it is evenly covered with seasonings and has wilted to the desired texture.

6. Remove the kale from the heat and enjoy!

Sweet Treats

Aren't we all addicted to sweets! The difference here is that all of these recipes use natural sweeteners and are totally guilt free!

       Berry Nice Cream...................................72
       Sweet Rolls..75
       Date Snickers..76
       Coco Dates.. 77

Berry Nice Cream

Serves 2

This sweet treat has the texture of ice cream with a sweet and fruity flavor. Enjoy this treat on a warm summer day.

Ingredients
2 frozen bananas
1/2 cup fresh raspberries
1/8 cup fresh blueberries
2 tbsp agave syrup

Directions
1. Toss all of the ingredients into a blender.

2. Blend the ice cream on the lowest setting until all of the ingredients are evenly combined.

3. Remove and enjoy with your choice of toppings.

Tips

For a thicker texture, freeze the ice cream for about 1-2 more hours

Sweet Rolls

Serves 4

These raw treats are so good that nobody will believe they aren't cooked. Satisfy your sweet tooth with these naturally sweet rolls.

Ingredients
8 dates
1 cup of almonds
1/2 cup of coconut flakes
1 pinch of pink himalayan salt
1/2 tsp of cinnamon
1/4 tsp of ginger
1/4 tsp nutmeg
1/8th cup of agave syrup

Directions
1. Pit the dates (remove the seed) and place them into a small container. Fill the container with warm water and cover it for about 5-10 minutes.

2. Blend the almonds, coconut flakes, cinnamon, nutmeg, and ginger in a food processor. Remove the powdered product and place it into a large bowl.

3. Place the dates and agave syrup into the food processor and blend until it creates a smooth and stick texture. Use a spoon or spatula to scoop out it out of the blender and then place it into the large bowl with the dry ingredients.

4. Stir the dry and wet ingredients together to form one large sticky substance similar to dough. Use a teaspoon to scoop out the sweet dough and form it into balls.

5. Roll each ball in coconut flakes.

6. There is no baking required, eat the ball as is.

Date Snickers — Serves 5

This plant-based interpretation of the Snickers bars you grew up with are to die for! Share these sweet treats with your family and friends!

Ingredients
1/2 cup dairy-free chocolate chips
14 medjool dates
2 tbsp olive oil
3 tbsp peanut butter
1/4 cup of nuts

Directions
1. Slice one side of each date and remove the seed.

2. Use a knife to fill each date with peanut butter and then place 1-2 peanuts inside. After the date has been filled press it together to close it.

3. Set all of the dates to the side to prepare the chocolate dip.

4. Combine the chocolate chips with your cooking oil, and use either a microwave or pot to melt the chocolate.

5. Dip each date in the chocolate and then allow it to cool at room temperature.

Coco Dates
Serves 5

This treat is a plant-based interpretation of the Mounds bars. It is covered in rich dairy free dark chocolate, so a little bit will go a long way.

Ingredients
1/2 cup dairy free chocolate chips
14 medjool dates
2 tbsp olive oil
1/4 cup coconut flakes

Directions
1. Slice one side of each date and remove the seed.

2. Fill each date with as much coconut flakes as you can.

3. Combine the chocolate chips, cooking oil, and use either a microwave or pot to melt the chocolate.

4. Dip each date in the chocolate and allow it to cool at room temperature.

Indulge

If you are partaking in the weight-loss program, you can enjoy these scrumptious meals once every week. There's no reason to go back to animal foods when you can enjoy these amazingly scrumptious plant-based recipes.

Apple & Date Oatmeal	80
Veggie Toast	83
Veggie Sub	84
Veggie Quesadilla	87
Bella Burger	88
Panang Curry Vegetables	90
Caribbean Asian Fusion Stir-Fry	91

Apple & Date Oatmeal

Serves 1

This sweet and savory oatmeal is irresistible. Each bowl is full of fiber and bold flavors!

Ingredients
2 dates
1/2 apple
coconut oil, as needed
2 tbsp agave syrup
1 tsp cinnamon
1 dash nutmeg
1 pinch fresh ginger
1 cup water
1/2 cup rolled oats
1 banana

Directions

1. Remove the pit from the dates. Slice the apple and dates to desired size.

2. Pour enough oil into a small pot to thinly coat its bottom and place the pot over low heat. Add cinnamon, nutmeg, and agave syrup. Stir frequently to create an evenly mixed sauce.

3. Add the sliced apples to the mixture and cover with a lid. Cook the apples for about 4-5 minutes or until tender.

4. Add dates to the mixture shortly after the apples have begun to soften. Cover the pot and allow the mixture to simmer.

5. Pour enough water into another small pot over high heat. Slice the banana while you wait for the water to reach a boil. Once the water reaches a boil, add the oatmeal and sliced bananas.

6. Stir the mixture for about 30 seconds. Turn the stove down to low heat and allow the oatmeal to simmer for about 5-7 minutes or until it has reach its desired texture.

7. Serve the oatmeal in a bowl, topped with the apple and date mixture. Garnish your dish with your choice of nuts and additional toppings. Enjoy!

Tips

Texture Tips. Cook less time for a thinner consistency and longer for a thicker consistency.

Veggie Toast

Serves 2

This spin on the open-faced sandwich is the perfect blend of savory and sweet. Enjoy this delicious meal in the morning with a warm cup of herbal tea.

Ingredients
1/2 green pepper
1/2 yellow onion
1/2 ripe plantain
grapeseed oil, as needed
water, as needed
1 tsp Mrs. Dash Garlic and Herb Seasoning
1/2 tsp pink himalayan salt
1/2 tsp freshly ground black pepper
1 handful kale
2 slices of bread Ezekiel, whole grain, or whole-wheat, toasted

Directions

1. Slice the green pepper, onion, and plantain to the desired thickness.

2. Pour enough oil into a large pan to thinly coat its bottom and place the pan over medium heat. Warm the oil until it is hot enough to fry the plantain slices.

3. Gently lay the plantain slices into the hot oil, making sure not to crowd the slices, and cook for about 3-4 minutes on each side, or until they are a dark brown color. Transfer the plantains to a paper-towel lined plate to drain and cool. Repeat until all slices are cooked, and remove from the heat.

4. Pour enough water into a medium-sized pan to thinly coat its bottom and place the pan over medium-high heat. Add the garlic and herb seasoning, salt, and black pepper and bring to a light boil.

5. Add the pepper and onion to the pot and cook at a steady light boil for about 2-3 minutes, or until the onion becomes translucent. Add the spinach and cook until the spinach as wilted. Remove from the heat.

6. Serve this delectable meal by placing the toasted bread on a serving plate. Top with the cooked veggies and plantains and enjoy!

Tips

Sweet or Savory? Add your favorite jelly for extra sweetness or guacamole for extra savoriness

Got Plantain? Save the extra plantain for your curry salad or eat them as a snack.

Veggie Sub

Serves 2

This sandwich is super simple and packed with tons of different flavors. You'll easily get a variety of veggies in your diet with this quick and easy meal.

Ingredients
multi-grain submarine roll, as needed
1 handful kale
1/4 onion
1/2 pepper (color of choice)
1/4 tomato
3 tbsp guacamole or avocado
1/2 tsp pink himalayan salt
1 dash cayenne pepper
1/2 tsp black pepper
1/2 tsp oregano

Directions
1. Slice loaf of bread to preferred size.

2. Spread guacamole onto both sides of the bread.

3. Chop all of the fresh vegetables to the desired size. Add the vegetables to the sandwich.

4. Sprinkle salt, pepper, and oregano onto your sandwich. Add cayenne pepper for an extra kick of spice

Tips

Need Fresh Guac? See page 64 for homemade guacamole recipe.

Want something cooked? Grill your favorite vegetables and add them to this sandwich.

Veggie Quesadilla
Serves 3

Quesadillas were a staple in my house during my college days! After making the switch to a plant-based diet, I remade this recipe without the cheese, and it still tastes incredible! Try it out!

Ingredients
2 bell peppers
2 cloves of garlic
1 small yellow onion
2 handfuls mushrooms
water, as needed
2 tsp of Jamaican jerk rub
1 tsp Mrs. Dash garlic and herb
1/4 tsp pink himalayan salt
1/2 tsp black pepper
1 dash paprika
2 handfuls spinach
grapeseed oil, as needed
4-5 tortilla shells
salsa, as needed
guacamole, as needed

Directions

1. Slice the peppers, onion, mushroom, and garlic to desired size.

2. Pour enough water into a large pan to thinly coat its bottom and place the pan over medium heat.

3. Add garlic, onion, and seasonings to the pan and allow it to reach a light boil.

4. Add peppers and mushrooms to the pan and cook them for about 5 minutes or until they have reached desired tenderness.

5. Add spinach into the pan and cook until the spinach has wilted. Remove the vegetables from the heat.

6. Pour a small amount of oil into a frying pan to barely coat its bottom and place the pan over medium heat.

7. Allow the oil to warm up until it moves freely like a loose liquid and covers the entire pan.

8. Add a tortilla shell into the pan and allow each side to cook for about 1-2 minutes.

9. Add the desired amount of vegetables to one side of the quesadilla. Fold the empty half of the quesadilla onto the side covered in vegetables and press it down firmly using a spatula.

10. Allow the quesadilla to cook for about 2-4 minutes. Flip using the spatula and allow the other side to cook for the same amount of time. Continue to press it down firmly so that it sticks together.

11. Remove the quesadilla from the heat and serve with your choice of salsa or guacamole.

Bella Burger

Serves 3

This juicy mushroom burger will easily satisfy your burger cravings. It's super tasty and significantly lower in calories in comparison to a beef or turkey burger!

Ingredients
3 large portabello mushrooms
2 cloves garlic
2 tbsp balsamic vinegar
1 tbsp grapeseed oil
1 1/2 tsp Montreal steak seasoning
1/2 green pepper
1/2 onion
cooking oil, as needed
water, as needed
1 tsp Mrs. Dash garlic and herb seasoning
1/2 tsp pink himalayan salt
1/2 tsp black pepper
1 handful spinach
3 whole wheat Hamburger buns
Cast iron grill

Directions
1. Clean the mushrooms, remove the stem, and use a spoon to scrape out the gills underneath the cap of the mushroom.

2. Create the burger sauce by chopping the garlic cloves and mixing it together with the balsamic vinegar, olive oil, and Montreal steak seasoning in a small mixing bowl.

3. Use a basting brush to spread the sauce evenly on each side of the mushrooms. Allow the mushrooms to marinate for about 10 minutes. Create another batch of the sauce to use for later.

4. Slice the green peppers and onions to desired thickness.

5. Evenly coat the cast iron grill skillet with cooking oil and place it over medium heat. Cook the mushrooms on each side for about 7-10 minutes or until it has reached desired tenderness. Use the basting brush to add additional sauce to the burger while it is cooking. Periodically cover the skillet while the mushrooms cook to preserve its moisture.

6. In a separate pan, pour enough water to lightly cover its bottom and place over medium heat. Add pink Himalayan salt, black pepper, and garlic and herb seasoning. Allow the water to reach a light boil, and then add the peppers and onions. Cook the veggies until they have reached desired tenderness. Add spinach and continue to cook the vegetables until they have willed.

7. Remove the mushrooms patties and vegetables from the heat.

8. Toast the hamburger buns until they have reached desired texture.

9. Slice the tomato and avocado to desired thickness.

10. Serve these delicious burgers by placing each patty on a bun and topping with cooked veggies, fresh tomato, and avocado slices. Add additional toppings of choice to please your taste buds and enjoy!

Panang Curry

Serves 4

I'll admit it: I stole this recipe from my dad. After I introduced him to a plant-based lifestyle, he surprised us all with his cooking skills. His vegan Panang Curry is so savory and delicious, I had to share it with you!

Ingredients

2 cups jasmine rice
3-4 cloves garlic
1 sweet potato
1 red potato
2 yellow onions
2 bell peppers
1 cup broccoli
1/2 cup mushrooms
1/2 cup carrots
grapeseed oil, as needed
Small handful thyme
1 tbsp Jamaican curry powder
1 jar Double Golden Fish Brand red instant curry paste
2 cans of coconut milk
1 dash pink himalayan salt
2 handfuls of snap peas

Directions

1. Prepare 2 cups of rice. Refer to the cooking instructions on the package.

2. Slice garlic, sweet potatoes, carrots, onions, mushrooms, peppers, and broccoli to desired size.

3. Add enough coconut oil to a large pot to thinly coat its bottom, and place over medium heat. Add garlic, thyme, and Jamaican curry powder. Stir frequently until fragrant.

4. Add the jar of Thai red curry paste to the pot. Stir the mixture until the red paste darkens.

5. Shake the coconut milk before use, and add both cans into the pot.

6. Stir vigorously until the sauce is evenly mixed. Add potatoes, carrots, and 1 dash of salt to the mixture. Cook for about 10-15 minutes.

7. Add the remaining veggies to the pot and cook on medium heat covered for 8-10 minutes or until the vegetables have reached the desired texture.

8. Remove the vegetables and rice from the heat, serve, and enjoy!

Tips

Try a healthier grain! Substitute the rice for barley.

Carubbean Vegetable Stir-Fry
Serves 5

The theft continues; I stole this recipe from my mom. It's been a staple in our home —in fact, it was one of our first home-cooked plant-based meals. Why order take out when you can make it yourself?

Ingredients
1/2 box Ronzoni 100% Whole Gran Noodle
2 tbsp vegetable oil
2 tbsp fresh garlic
1 12oz Smart Food Stir fry vegetables (broccoli, snow peas, carrots, and red cabbage)
2 bell peppers
1 onion
1 pack of whole portabello mushroom
1 cup cabbage
2 tsp onion powder
1 tbsp walker wood Jamaican jerk seasoning
1/2 bottle House of Tsang General Tsao Sauce

Directions
1. Boil noodles according to package instructions.

2. Slice vegetables to preferred size.

3. Heat vegetable oil in a wok or large pan over medium/high heat.

3. Add chopped garlic to the pan and allow it to saute without burning for 2-3 minutes.

4. Add stir fry vegetables, peppers, onion, and portabello mushrooms to the pan and cook for about 7 minutes.

5. Add cabbage to the pan and cook the vegetables for an additional 5 minutes.

6. Add onion powder and walker wood seasoning, and stir the mixture. Allow it to cook on low heat for an additional 3 minutes.

7. Add noodles and Tsagn General Tsao sauce to the vegetables, and allow it to cook for 3 more minutes.

8. Remove the pasta from the heat and serve.

Additional Information

    In this final section, I share the reasons why I try to eat organic foods as often as possible, and also a list of resources that inspired me to pursue a plant-based diet. Thank you so much for making it this far into the book, and I encourage you to explore this topic in more detail. It's my hope that I've inspired you to do your own research and work to improve both your health and the world we all live in!

Why I Try to Eat Organic

What are GMO Foods? "GMO" stands for genetically modified organisms. In corporate reports prepared by Monsanto's website, GMO foods are defined as "plants or animals that have had their genetic makeup altered to exhibit traits that are not naturally theirs."[9]

These organisms are produced through the act of transgenic gene-splicing techniques. Essentially, the genes of different organisms are spliced together, removing a desirable gene from one organism and placing it into another. This relatively new scientific technology allows DNA from one species to be transferred to another.

Why avoid them? These foods are unsafe simply because they aren't natural. Nature's beautiful cycles are perfect and never wasteful. At the cellular level, our bodies go through a constant cycle of death and rebirth—replacing about 1 percent of all cells each day, which adds up to 30 percent of all cells each month, and 100 percent each season. The new cells we create are largely made up of the nutrients we ingest through our food. So if we disrupt our bodies' natural cycles by ingesting unnatural foods, the new cells formed by these foods are also unnatural—and at risk for developing disease. This is why I don't trust genetically modified foods. They're simply too new for us to truly understand how they affect our health and the health of further generations.

How can you make a difference? Ever since GMO foods hit the market about 20 years ago, we've been left in the dark. The government does not require them to be labeled, so we have no idea if we are eating GMO or naturally grown foods. In my opinion it's simply ridiculous that we cannot make informed food choices. If you think GMO foods should be labeled in your state, check out the website www.justlabelit.com—it's a remarkable resource that can link you to petitions you can sign to make a difference. Demand control of your food rights!

Do Your Own Research

The documentaries and websites listed below inspired me to commit to a mainly plant-based lifestyle. I've also added there release years to help you distinguish between the documentaries with the latest research. Enjoy!

Name	Year
What the Health	(2017)
Feel Rich	(2017)
What's With Wheat	(2016)
Food Choices	(2016)
Sustainable	(2016)
Plant Pure Nation	(2015)
Sugar Coated	(2015)
Fed Up	(2014)
Cowspiracy	(2014)
Fat, Sick, and Nearly Dead 2	(2014)
Live and let Live	(2013)
GMO OMG	(2013)
Hungry For Change	(2012)
Forks Over Knives	(2011)
Vegucated	(2010)
Fat, Sick, and Nearly Dead	(2010)
Food Inc	(2008)
Earthlings	(2005)

Additional Resources

nutritionfacts.org

nutritionstudies.org

References

[1] https://www.niddk.nih.gov/health-information/health-statistics/overweight-obesity

[2] https://www.cdc.gov/obesity/data/adult.html

[3] US Department of Agriculture (USDA). Dietary Guidelines for Americans 2015–2020, Eighth Edition. https://health.gov/dietaryguidelines/2015/resources/2015-2020_Dietary_Guidelines.pdf

[4] https://www.cdc.gov/mmwr/preview/mmwrhtml/mm6426a1.htm

[5] Nurses' Health Study and Health Professionals Follow-up Study. https://content.sph.harvard.edu/hpfs/

[6] https://nutritionfacts.org/topics/plant-based-diets/

[7] Tuso, P., Ismail, M., Ha, B. and Bartolotto, C. (2015). Nutritional Update for Physicians: Plant-Based Diets. [online] The Permanente Journal. Available at: https://doi.org/10.7812/TPP/12-085 [Accessed 8 Nov. 2017].

Grateful Heart

My biggest thanks goes out to all of my family and friends who have seen me throughout the creation of this book. Thank you all for being supportive and positive throughout this roller coaster ride of a journey. Thank you for pushing me to complete this book and to further live out my dreams. Thank you to all of the individuals in my life, known and unknown, who sincerely believed in me, prayed for me, and wished the best for me.

Thank you to my father and photographer for patiently capturing all of these images. You have truly helped me bring my book to life!

Thank you to my mother, for being my taste tester. Thank you for always being honest with me about each recipe. Even when the critiques were not something that I wanted to hear, they were always something that I needed to hear. You have really helped me improve my cooking skills.

Thank you to my aunts, grandparents, friends, god parents, and play-aunties for always supporting me. Thank you for telling all of your friends about me, and spreading my message of a healthier lifestyle.

Thank you Zach Rogers, for always being positive and reminding me that I am 90% done, even when the 10% seemed impossible and was stressing me out.

Thank you Taylor Walton for reading my entire book and sending me edits. You are literally a lifesaver and an amazing friend!

Thank you to my teachers, in school and outside of school, for providing me with this knowledge to share with others. Although our time may have been short, and conversations few and far in between, I truly appreciate the knowledge that you have shared with me.

And last but not least, the warmest and sincerest thanks goes to you! This book would be nothing without your support. Thank you for purchasing this book, supporting me, and joining me on this journey to the healthiest and best versions of ourselves.

With Love,
Janae Horton

About The Author

Janae Horton is a Certified Health Coach, Nutritionist, member of the American Nutrition Association, and CEO of Live incorporated. After obtaining a Bachelors of Science degree in Nutrition Science from the University of Georgia, Janae furthered her education by receiving a Certification in Health Coaching from Emory University. Janae's nutrition education combined with coaching techniques has enabled her to educate, connect with, and empower clients to release negative habits and foods that have hindered their health and wellness journey.

Janae has mastered the art of facilitating her clients' progressive development through active listening, motivational interviewing, and client-centered goal setting. Her passion to see her clients succeed allows her to empathize with each individual and provide them with a coaching plan that is specifically tailored to fit their needs. Janae has a proven track record of facilitating client progression in its many forms: physical, mental, and emotional. For these reasons, Janae has developed this resource guide filled with nutrition information, weight-loss guide, and recipes to spread her nutrition expertise to those in need.

Made in the USA
Columbia, SC
24 March 2019